GW00703286

Kent Buses
In Camera

by
Philip C. Miles

QUOTES LIMITED

MCMXCV

Published by Quotes Limited
Whittlebury, England

Typeset in Plantin by
Key Composition, Northampton, England

Pictures Lithographed by
South Midlands Lithoplates Limited, Luton, England

Printed by Busiprint Limited
Buckingham, England

Bound by WBC Bookbinders Limited
Bridgend, Glamorgan

ISBN 0 86023 625 0

Acknowledgements

I would like to thank the following people and organisations for their invaluable assistance in the preparation of this book: the Maidstone & District and East Kent Bus Club for help in the history of the companies, the East Pennine Bus Group, Mr G. W. H. Dodson, Mr Roy Marshall, the late Mr Robert F. Mack and again the Maidstone & District and East Kent Bus Club for supplying me with such excellent photographs, many reproduced from the companies' collections, while others are from their own private collections.

It is impractical to include every operator or every type of vehicle so I have concentrated on the three main operators in the Kent area: Maidstone & District, East Kent Road Car and Maidstone Corporation. Another book on Kent will contain independents.

This volume shows through photographs how road transport has changed over the last hundred years, from the electric tram, through char-a-bancs to the modern day 'buses.

Key to photographers
RFM   Mr Robert F. Mack
GWHD   Mr G. W. H. Dodson
RM   Mr Roy Marshall
MD&EKBC   Maidstone & District and East Kent Bus Club

Dedication

This book is dedicated with love to my Mother

FRONT COVER: *Several different types of bus were purchased in the early years of Maidstone & District; one such was KT 516, a Daimler 40hp built in 1913. (MD&EKBC)*

A number of tramway operations were established early on in Kent, including the Gravesend and Northfleet Tramways, the Chatham & District Tramways, Dover Corporation Tramways and the Isle of Thanet Electric Supply Co. Maidstone Corporation Tramways commenced on 14 July 1904, after gaining a Light Railway Order in 1903 allowing the Corporation to operate trams. The first route was from the High Street to Barming, extended in October 1907 to Loose, while a further tram route was opened to Tovil, on 9 January 1908.

Numerous small operators using char-a-bancs or early motorbuses also operated and the first known service commenced in 1903 at Folkestone. In the East Kent area the London & South Coast Motor Company was registered on 17 November 1905, while the East Kent and Herne Bay Motor Omnibus Co was formed in September 1905. In 1908 an omnibus services was operated by the Maidstone, Chatham, Gravesend Omnibus Services, running vehicles during the day as 'buses and at night fitted with lorry bodies to carry such things as local farm produce to Covent Garden Market! In 1908 a motorbus service was operated in the Deal area by Sidney Garcke, (of the BET founding family) who began other services as far away as Canterbury and Herne Bay with the fleetname Deal & District Motor Services. In 1910 the undertaking was transferred to the British Automobile Development Co Ltd. Other small motorbus firms quickly opened up routes. Mr W. F. French was a pioneer of early motorbuses in the Isle of Thanet; French who had taken an interest in the firm of Strong's Garage and Motor Car Co Ltd, had started in 1908 — from his cycle shop. After French had taken an interest a new title was used — French, Banister & Co Ltd; that developed services in the Margate area and the name was once again changed in July 1914 to the Margate, Canterbury & District Motor Services Ltd.

On 22 March 1911 Maidstone & District Motor Services was formed, as the successor to Maidstone, Chatham & District Motor Omnibus Services. The first routes operated were between Maidstone and Chatham and between Gravesend and Chatham. After the 1st World War Maidstone & District Motor Services quickly acquired other operators, including in 1920 a subsidiary of the Gravesend & Northfleet Electric Tramways Ltd, the North Kent Motor Services Ltd. Buck's Motor Services of Maidstone and Red Road Cars of Lenham were taken over in 1929.

In 1914, the well-known London-based operator, Thomas Tilling Ltd, began operating services in the Folkestone area, trading as the Folkestone & District Road Car Company. On 11 August 1916 East Kent Road Car Co Ltd was registered and commenced operation on 1 September 1916. The companies which formed East Kent were the Folkestone & District Road Car Company, Deal & District Motor Services, the Margate, Canterbury & District Motor Services Ltd, H. B. Wacher & Co Ltd of Herne Bay and Ramsgate Motor Coaches (Griggs) Ltd. In 1928 East Kent became part of the TBAT group, while the Southern Railway purchased an interest in the company.

Maidstone Corporation Tramways commenced 'bus operation on 7 April 1924, with five Tilling-Stevens single deck 'buses, numbers 1-5 (KK9418-20 and KL1650-51). The first route was between London Road and Penenden Heath. After obtaining the necessary Act, trolleybuses were introduced in Maidstone using eight Ransome D6s with Ransome 62-seat bodies, while the Barming tram route was converted in May 1928. Further motorbus and trolleybus services were introduced in the late 1920s and early 1930s. Trams ceased operations on 11 February 1929.

In 1930, the Southern Railway acquired an interest in the East Kent fleet under the powers granted to it in 1928, while in 1937 East Kent Road Car took over the Isle of Thanet Electric Supply Company and Dover Corporation Tramways, converting them to 'bus operation. The Southern Railway also took an interest in Maidstone & District while, like East Kent, Maidstone & District took over several tramway operations; the Gravesend & Northfleet Tramway was acquired in 1929 and replaced by motorbuses. It later passed to the newly formed London Passenger Transport Board in 1933, while the Chatham Tramway closed on 30 September 1930, replaced by Maidstone & District motorbuses, using the fleetname Chatham & District, who continued as a subsidiary of Maidstone & District until 1955.

Both East Kent Road Car and Maidstone & District Motor Services continued to acquire other companies, Maidstone & District buying Autocar Services Ltd of Tunbridge Wells and Redcar Services, also of Tunbridge Wells. East Kent Road Car acquired the London & South Coast Motor Services.

Maidstone Corporation Transport continued to expand its trolleybus system up to 1963 alongside new housing developments. However, trolleybuses in the end gave way to the motorbus and the last day of trolleybus operation in Maidstone was 15 April 1967.

In 1969, Maidstone & District Motor Services and East Kent Road Car Company became part of the National Bus Company — both operators had been under BET control since 1942, though second generation George French continued to direct the business for many years. (The publisher's father, Raymond W. Birch CBE, chaired East Kent within BET). After deregulation both East Kent Road Car and Maidstone & District Motor Services were bought out by management, East Kent on 5 March 1987 and Maidstone & District on 6 November 1986. East Kent is now a member of the Stagecoach group, while Boro'line (Maidstone Corporation's new name) was put up for sale in 1991. Maidstone & District competed with Boro'line in December 1991, Boro'line fell into administrative receivership on 19 February 1992 and its last day of 'bus operation was 29 May 1992, ending ninety years of Maidstone Corporation Transport.

Tramway operation commenced in Maidstone in 1904. Six ERTCW cars with 48-seat open-tops were bought. Car number 1 is seen on the original tram route to Barming. (MD&EKBC)

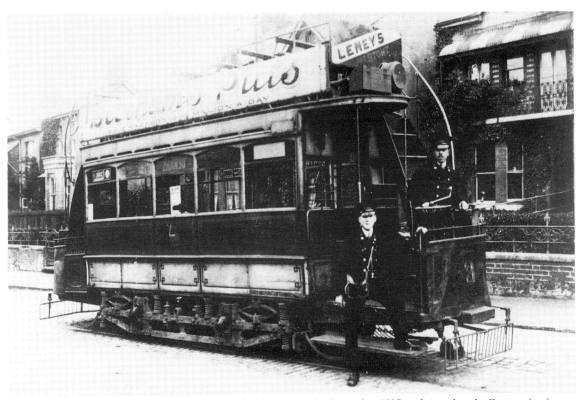

Electric tramways started in Dover under private ownership in September 1897 and passed to the Corporation in November 1904. The motorman and conductor pose with Dover Corporation Tramways car number 3, an open-top and open-staircase double-deck car. East Kent Road Car took over operations in January 1937 and replaced them with 'buses. (MD&EKBC)

Ten more double-deck open-top cars were purchased in 1907 by Maidstone Corporation Tramways for the opening of a new tram route to Loose. These were UECs with seating for 40. One of the cars is number 12. (MD&EKBC)

This early Halford double-deck 'bus was in the fleet of Maidstone, Chatham, Gravesend & District Motor Services. It is thought to be D3449, new in 1908, one of the first to operate between Maidstone and Chatham. It was photographed at Rose Yard Mews, Maidstone c1908. (MD&EKBC)

Maidstone & District Motor Services was formed on 22 March 1911. The fleet consisted of just five vehicles, one of them D4501, a Halford 24-seat char-a-banc with solid tyres. (MD&EKBC)

Maidstone & District Motor Services operated this Daimler 40hp, new in 1913. It is thought to be KT 873.
(MD&EKBC)

In 1915, Maidstone & District Motor Services purchased KT 6415, one of two Straker Squire double-deck 'buses with bodywork by Tillings. KT 6415 is seen with a display board for one of the original routes operated by Maidstone & District. (MD&EKBC)

FN 3749, a Tilling Stevens TS3, was purchased by East Kent Road Car along with several other Tilling Stevens in 1919. FN 3749 shows the early style of bodywork fitted to saloons, in this case by Palmer, with a seating capacity for twenty-nine. Note the additional nearside door to the luggage area and emergency exit. (MD&EKBC)

This Leyland O was fitted with a Harrington char-a-banc body. KE 9791 was also fitted with the luxury of pneumatic tyres, and was once operated by Maidstone & District Motor Services. It was built in 1922.
(MD&EKBC)

Maidstone Corporation Transport started 'bus services in 1924, with five Tilling Stevens. One of them is number 4 (KL 1650) a TS6, with Tilling Stevens B36D body. (RM)

In 1924, a number of Tilling Stevens were added to the Maidstone & District fleet, including KL 1551, a TS3A with a Tilling 51-seat open-top body. KL 1551 is outside the Gillingham depôt on service 1 to Maidstone. (MD&EKBC)

Maidstone & District KL 4204 is a Tilling Stevens TS6 petrol-electric and carries a Tilling 51-seat open-top body, new in 1925. (MD&EKBC)

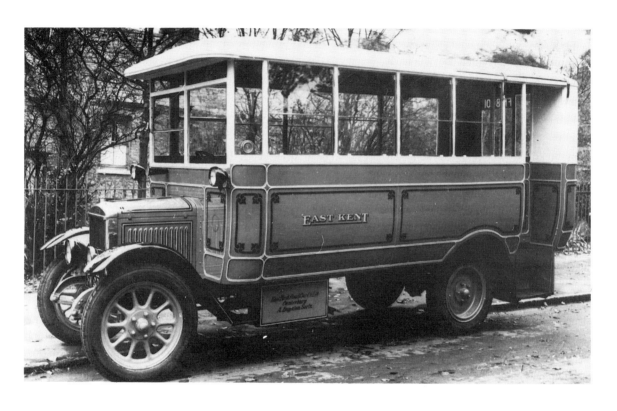

East Kent Road Car added twelve Morris 1-ton vehicles with East Kent 14-seat bodywork to the fleet in 1926, including FN 8001. (MD&EKBC)

Maidstone Corporation Transport number 8 (KM3939) is a Tilling-Stevens LL with a Beadle B36C entrance body, new in 1926. It is photographed on the Hackney Road service. (MD&EKBC)

In 1925, a large number of Tilling-Stevens were purchased by Maidstone & District, with bodywork by Short, Harrington & Beadle. Number 492 (KP 3020), a Tilling B9A, carries a Beadle B31R body. (MD&EKBC)

The last Tilling-Stevens were purchased by Maidstone Corporation Transport in 1928 — two B10As with Vickers B32R bodies. One is number 9 (KP 319), seen here when new. (RM)

A number of Tilling-Stevens B10D2s were added to the East Kent Road Car fleet in 1929, including FN 9949, with Short C30R touring bodies. These were 'all-weather' vehicles — the roof could be removed when required but FN 9949 is seen here with it in place. (MD&EKBC)

East Kent Road Car JG 655, dating from 1930, was a Leyland TS1 with a Short open-top 56-seat body. It has a rear outside staircase and is pictured at Ramsgate Harbour. The body was scrapped in February 1945 and a new single-deck 34-seat utility body by Burlingham was fitted. This vehicle was finally withdrawn in 1949. (GWHD)

The first Leyland Titans for the East Kent Road Car fleet arrived in 1930: JG 977/8, JG 1057/8, JG 1411/2 with Leyland L27/24R bodies. JG 977 is seen shortly after delivery on the outskrits of Dover on an official outing. (MD&EKBC)

This is believed to be JG 1623, delivered to East Kent Road Car in 1931, with the third batch of Leyland TD1s for the company, with Leyland 51-seat bodies. It is in Margate on service 46 to Minnis Bay, and was loaned to Venture, Basingstoke from 1940 to May 1942, when it went straight to Cumberland Motor Services until June 1943. It was withdrawn in 1947. (GWHD)

East Kent Road Car JG 1477 is a 1931 Morris Commercial Viceroy and fitted with this Beadle B20F body.
(MD&EKBC)

In 1932, Maidstone & District purchased twenty-eight Leyland Titan TD2s with Leyland H24/24R bodies. One of the batch is number 181 (KJ 5446). (RM)

Maidstone & District Motor Services purchased eight Leyland Titan TD3s with Harrington front-entrance bodies, fitted with 48 coach seats, new in 1934. One of the eight is number 343, (BKK 307). (MD&EKBC)

East Kent Road Car JG 5431 and 5433 Leyland TS7s, dating from 1935, were two of 38 delivered that year. The original bodies were either destroyed by enemy action in September 1940 (JG 5433) or transferred to another coach which had been destroyed at the same time (JG 5431). Both then received new Park Royal 32-seat coach bodies in 1941, but with roof compartments for the carriage of musical instruments for military bands in the area. They were withdrawn in 1957 and are pictured at Tankerton (Whitstable). (GWHD)

Maidstone & District Motor Services number 583 (CKE 422), a Leyland TS7 with a Harrington C31F body, was one of twenty-one such delivered in 1935. (RM)

In 1936 East Kent turned to Dennis for the provision of single deck vehicles, with 23 Lancets; three Lancet 2s completed the order. Deliveries of Lancet 2s continued in 1937 with a further 25, all except the last bodied by Dennis. In the post-war rebuilding programme, JG 8712 received a new Park Royal 35-seat 'bus body in 1949. It lasted a further eight years. JG 8712 is here at Canterbury depôt. (GWHD)

In 1938, East Kent took delivery of JG 9907-9931, Leyland TD5s. JG 9907-18 had Park Royal L27/26R bodies, while JG 9919-9931 had Brush L27/26R bodies. One of the Brush examples is JG 9922, seen passing the West Gate Towers in Canterbury. This vehicle received a new Eastern Coachworks L26/28R body in 1948. (PCMC)

In 1938, two Crossley Mancunians with Crossley H24/24R bodies were added to the Maidstone Corporation Transport fleet. Number 42 (FKL 901) is photographed on the Tovil service. The seating capacity was altered in 1951 and they became H28/24R. (RM)

In 1939, East Kent took delivery of a further 20 Dennis Lancet 2s, of which the last 15 had Dennis 35-seat 'bus bodies. AJG 58, the last but one, survived until 1954. It is pictured at the Central Body Works. (GWHD.

Maidstone Corporation Transport purchased four Crossley Mancunians with Crossley 46-seat rear-entrance bodies in 1940. One of the four is number 47 (GKK 986). They were fitted with Gardner 5LW engines by Pelican Engineering in 1951 and the seating increased to 52 in 1951. (MD&EKBC)

In 1943, East Kent Road Car purchased seven utility Park Royal H30/26R Guy Arab Mark I and IIs. BJG 281 is an Arab II. Note the masked out front headlamps. (MD&EKBC)

A number of Daimlers were bought by Maidstone & District in 1943, along with Guy Arabs. This is a Daimler CWA6, with an utility Weymann 56-seat body. DH32 (GKP 8) received a new Waymann 56-seat body in 1951. (PCMC)

Maidstone Corporation Transport took delivery of three Sunbeam W trolleybuses with Park Royal H30/26R bodies in 1944. One of the batch is number 56 (GKP 511). This vehicle received a new Roe H34/28R body in 1960. It was withdrawn seven years later, and is now preserved. (RFM)

A number of 'bus operators took delivery of the utility-bodied Guy Arab during the Second World War. These were basic, with straight uncurved panels, which saved many hours of panel beating. This Guy Arab II has a Park Royal 56-seat rear-entrance body. Number 61 (HKJ 480) in the Maidstone Corporation Transport fleet, it was new in 1945, withdrawn from passenger service fourteen years later and converted to a breakdown wagon. It remained with Maidstone Borough Council until 1974. (PCMC)

Delivered to East Kent Road Car in 1945, this Weymann utility 56-seat bodied Guy Arab II 6LW, BJG 472 was converted to open-top in 1959 and remained with East Kent until withdrawn ten years later. Holidaymakers enjoy the fresh air on the coastal service to Palm Bay. (RFM)

Trolleybuses 62-67 (HKR 1-6) were Sunbeam W4s with NCB H30/26R bodies, added to the Maidstone Corporation Transport fleet in 1946. Number 67 is on the old tram route to Barming. (RFM)

Maidstone & District purchased DH163-199, Bristol Ks with Weymann H56R bodies, in 1946. Ex-number 180 (HKL 863) is a K6A. It was converted to open-top status in 1957 and became OT8. On the right is DH231 (JKM 928) of 1948, also a Bristol K6A but with a Saunders H56R body. (MD&EKBC)

In 1947, East Kent took delivery of a large number of Dennis Lancet J3s with Park Royal B35R bodies. In 1959 some of these vehicles were rebuilt by Park Royal to full front. The rear entrance was moved to the front and they were converted to one-man operation. CFN 130 was one such vehicle and remained in service until 1966. (MD&EKBC)

The first Daimlers for the Maidstone Corporation Transport fleet were purchased in 1947, when three CVG6s with NCB H30/26R bodies were taken into stock. Number 75 (JKO 639) is one. (RFM)

In 1948, twenty Leyland Titan PD1s with Leyland L27/26R bodies were purchased by East Kent Road Car, CJG 967-986; this is CJG 980. (PCMC)

In 1949, East Kent Road Car took delivery of this Dennis Falcon P3, with a Dennis B20F body. EFN 557 was one of a batch of five, fitted for one-man operation. EFN 557 had its seating capacity increased to 29 in 1957, and was withdrawn in 1965. (RFM)

Maidstone Corporation Transport purchased six Daimler CVG6s with Brush 56-seat rear-entrance bodies in 1949. One of the six is number 80 (LKJ 789); it remained with Maidstone Corporation until it was withdrawn in 1963. (PCMC)

A number of AEC Regals with either Beadle or Harrington coach bodies were purchased by Maidstone & District in 1949. Howerver, CO97 (KKK 836) was the only full-fronted coach. It carries a modern (for the year) Harrington 31-seat coach body. (MD&EKBC)

A number of operators purchased the Beadle rebuild vehicles in the early 1950s. Maidstone & District CO200 (MKT 800) was new in 1950, and carries a Beadle C35F body and used units from DH310, a 1935 AEC Regent. (MD&EKBC)

This Bristol LA6 carries a smart half-cab Eastern Coachworks B35R body. SO46 (LKT 994) was new to Maidstone & District in 1950. It is photographed on service 51 Ore via Sidley, and was one of thirteen purchased that year. (MD&EKBC)

FFN 382 in the East Kent fleet is a 1951 Guy Arab III 6LW fitted with a Park Royal 56-seat rear-entrance body. Alongside is GFN 931, a 1953 Guy Arab IV, also with a Park Royal 56-seat rear-entrance body, but fitted with platform doors. (MD&EKBC)

Three different chassis and coachwork builders were added to the East Kent fleet in 1952, including Leyland Royal Tiger PSU1/15 with Park Royal coachwork, Bedford SBs with Duple Vega coachwork and the semi-chassisless Leyland-Beadle with Beadle bodywork. FFN 449 is one of the Leyland Royal Tigers with Park Royal 30-seat central-entrance bodywork. This coach was one of three fitted with boat racks on the roof in 1965-6. (PCMC)

In 1952, fifteen Leyland Royal Tiger PSU1/15s were added to the Maidstone & District fleet. CO272-286; all but CO272 carried Leyland's attractive coach body. One of the batch is number C285, seen with its new fleetnumber after it was renumbered in 1961. (MD&EKBC)

For the coach fleet, East Kent purchased thirty Dennis Lancet UFs in 1954 and had them fitted with Duple Ambassador IV coachwork. HJG 3-8 were 32-seaters, while HJG 9-32 were 41-seaters. HJG 25 gave good service with East Kent, not withdrawn until 1970. (MD&EKBC)

In 1955, East Kent took delivery of thirty-nine AEC Reliances with Weymann DP41F and three Beadle-Commers with Beadle DP41F bodies. One of the latter is KFN 252, the last of the trio. (RM)

In 1957, three Leyland Titan PD2/30s with Massey H33/26R bodywork were taken into stock by Maidstone Corporation Transport. One of the three is number 7 (997 AKT). (RFM)

The last Guy Arabs purchased by East Kent were delivered in 1957, when fifteen Arab IV 6LWs with Park Royal H33/28R bodywork, fitted with platform doors, entered service. MFN 906 awaits passengers before setting off on route 13A. (MD&EKBC)

In 1956, fifteen Beadle-AEC rebuilds were added to the Maidstone & District fleet. Numbered CO360/373-376, (WKM 360 etc). Last of the batch is number CO376, using units from CO72, a 1948 AEC Regal III, with a Harrington coach body. With new 37-seat centre-entrance body, these vehicles had an extended life until 1964. (RM)

Maidstone & District purchased 32 AEC Reliances with bodywork by Beadle, Weymann and Harrington in 1957. SO234 (YKR 234) carries a Beadle B42F body. It was renumbered S234 in 1961 and in 1968 became 3234. (RFM)

Maidstone & District Motor Services was an early user of the Leyland Atlantean. DH525 (525 DKT) is a 1959 PDR1/1 with a Metro-Cammell body and 60 dual−purpose seats, while DH490-523 had 78 seats and the low height Atlanteans, with Weymann bodywork DK43-56, had seating for 73. DH525 was renumbered 5525 in 1968. (PCMC)

In 1959, Maidstone Corporation Transport acquired five Sunbeam W trolleybuses with Weymann H30/26R bodies from Maidstone & District Motor Services. These trolleybuses were new to the Hastings Tramway Company in 1947-8. One of them is number 89 (BDY 818) new in 1948, ex-Hastings number 43. (RFM)

Following PFN 843, an AEC Regent V with a Park Royal full-front 72-seat body, exhibited at the 1958 Commercial Motor Show, were 39 similar vehicles, delivered to East Kent in 1959, with PFN 844-882. PFN 852 shows the full-front design to good effect and is on service 51. (MD&EKBC)

Maidstone Corporation Transport number 13 (413 GKT) is a 1959 Leyland Titan PD2/30 with a Massey H33/26R body. Number 13 was one of three purchased that year, numbers 13-15. (RFM)

In 1959, East Kent took delivery of forty AEC Regent Vs with full-front 72-seat bodies by Park Royal. PFN 853 (originally allocated an OJG registration) went to the Thanet depôt, and was the first of this series to be converted to open-top in July 1972, when the company needed the extra capacity on the Thanet open-top service. (GWHD)

Maidstone & District Motor Services purchased fifteen Albion Nimbuses with Harrington 30-seat bodywork in 1960, for use on light or country routes. The driver of number 3318, ex-S318 (318 LKK), checks his ticket machine before his return journey on service 113. (MD&EKBC)

In 1961, Maidstone Corporation Transport took delivery of three attractive Massey-bodied Leyland Titan PD2A/30s with seating for 61. Number 18 (518 RKR) is seen here. (PCMC)

After the last full-fronted AEC Regents delivered in 1959, East Kent took delivery in 1961 of WFN 827-842, Regent Vs with Park Royal half-cab design and seating for 72. WFN 834 here shows the pleasing lines of the Park Royal body. (MD&EKBC)

East Kent took delivery of three AEC Bridgemasters with Park Royal H43/29F bodies in 1962. One of them is YJG 809, on a Dover town service. They were withdrawn in 1972, while the Regents delivered the same year stayed in service until 1976/7. (MD&EKBC)

Exhibited at the 1962 Commercial Motor Show — an AEC Reliance with a Willowbrook B54F body, number S1, (984 TKO) in the fleet of Maidstone & District. Along with other vehicles, this was renumbered in 1968 and became number 3701. (MD&EKBC)

In 1971, East Kent acquired from Southdown Motor Services 265-289 AUF and 100-104 CUF 1963 Leyland Leopard PSU3/1RTs, with Marshall B45F bodies. One of these is 267 AUF, ex-Southdown 667. It was withdrawn in 1975. (MD&EKBC)

A large number of AEC Reliances with Park Royal C49F or Marshall B51F bodywork were purchased in 1965 by East Kent Road Car — DJG 355-358C and DJG 606-631C. DJG 631C is one of the Park Royal vehicles and is photographed on the South Coast Express service X28. (RFM)

East Kent bought nothing but AEC Reliances for the single-deck fleet, for both coachwork and stage-carriage work between 1961 and 1966. One of the 1965 vehicles was DJG 356C with a Marshall 51-seat front-entrance body. This became number 1356 when fleet numbers were introduced in 1977. (MD&EKBC)

In 1965, Maidstone & District bought both AEC Reliances and Leyland Leopard single-deck 'buses, with bodywork by Marshall, Willowbrook and Weymann. SC44 (BKT 807C) is an AEC Reliance with an attractive Weymann 49-seat dual-purpose body. It is on the long run to Clacton on Sea. (MD&EKBC)

With trolleybus abandonment in 1967, Maidstone Corporation Transport bought eight Leyland Atlantean PDR1/1s with Massey H43/31F bodies. Atlantean number 41 (JKE 341E) is on one of the former trolleybus (and tram) routes. (RFM)

In 1967, East Kent replaced its ageing fleet of Dennis Falcons with a batch of Beford VASIs, with well-proportioned Marshall B29F bodywork. One of the batch is KJG 109E. This vehicle only lasted nine years with East Kent, withdrawn in 1976. (PCMC)

The first Willowbrook vehicles for East Kent entered service in 1968, when OJG 130-137F were purchased; these were AEC Reliances with 49 dual-purpose seats, used on express services and excursions. OJG 137F (later numbered 8137) is on service X32 to Clacton on Sea. (MD&EKBC)

In 1969, East Kent took on its first rear-engined double-deck 'buses, when RFN 953-972G entered the fleet; Daimler Fleetline CRG6LXs with Park Royal H39/31F bodywork. The last of the batch is RFN 972G, later given fleet number 7972. It is on service 25. (MD&EKBC)

East Kent took delivery in 1971 of eighteen AEC Reliances with Plaxton Coachwork and twelve AEC Swifts with Alexander B51F bodywork. YJG 590K is one of the Swifts. This vehicle became number 1590, and spent all its life at Dover. (MD&EKBC)

This Daimler Roadliner SRG6LX carries a Marshall 45-seat dual-doorway body. Number 3801 (SKO 801H) in the Maidstone & District fleet, it is photographed on the one-man operated route 65. New in 1970, it was sold to Northern General Transport in 1972. (MD&EKBC)

Index to Illustrations